icanhascheezburger?

HAS ZBURGER?

A LOLcat Colleckshun

**Professor Happycat
& icanhascheezburger.com**

GOTHAM
BOOKS

GOTHAM BOOKS
Published by Penguin Group (USA) Inc.
375 Hudson Street, New York, New York 10014, U.S.A.

Penguin Group (Canada), 90 Eglinton Avenue East, Suite 700, Toronto, Ontario M4P 2Y3, Canada (a division of Pearson
Penguin Canada Inc.); Penguin Books Ltd, 80 Strand, London WC2R 0RL, England; Penguin Ireland, 25 St Stephen's Green,
Dublin 2, Ireland (a division of Penguin Books Ltd); Penguin Group (Australia), 250 Camberwell Road, Camberwell, Victoria 3124,
Australia (a division of Pearson Australia Group Pty Ltd); Penguin Books India Pvt Ltd, 11 Community Centre, Panchsheel Park,
New Delhi - 110 017, India; Penguin Group (NZ), 67 Apollo Drive, Rosedale, North Shore 0632, New Zealand (a division of Pearson
New Zealand Ltd); Penguin Books (South Africa) (Pty) Ltd, 24 Sturdee Avenue, Rosebank, Johannesburg 2196, South Africa

Penguin Books Ltd, Registered Offices: 80 Strand, London WC2R 0RL, England

Published by Gotham Books, a member of Penguin Group (USA) Inc.

First printing, October 2008
10 9 8 7 6 5 4 3 2 1

Gotham Books and the skyscraper logo are trademarks of Penguin Group (USA) Inc.

LIBRARY OF CONGRESS CATALOGING-IN-PUBLICATION DATA has been applied for.

ISBN 978-1-592-40409-4

Printed in teh United States of America
Set in **IMPACT!!1!**
Designed bai Ben Gibson
Illustrations bai Lianne Uesato and Kenta Nemoto

No kittehs were harmd in teh making of dis book.

OH HAI

I BUFFED UR FLOOR

best

sock

evar

mai preshussss

MONORAIL CAT

MONORAIL CAT
ideel kitteh methud of travelng,
tho never on time and offen out
of servis

Monorail cat haz mrgncy airbrak

monorail kitteh

on lift for repares

EXPLAIN PLZ

im confusd

turn the gravity back on, ok ha?

Needs halp?

I canz do fotoshop

Naked Guy

reely freekin me owt

SPY CAM

installed and functioning

oh hai

been scratchin ur records

like a dj

i hope theyll be gone when i opens mah eyes

banker cat
denies ur
loan

a best friend... i has it

I has a job interview

cheezburger...

out dere...

sumwheres

banana fone

ringing off teh hook

greedy cat wants it all

emo kitteh

hates pretty things

grudge cat iz still ignoring u

financial advisor cat
disapprovs of ur banking methods

IN UR QUANTUM BOX...

...MAYBE.

gps cat

sez

u lost

for a brief shining moment
parrot thought he won

evr
hav
the
feelin

ur bein watched?

Hello from ebays!

not wut u xpected?

couch
kitteh

awaits ur arrival

lol

u peed ur pants

catini shaken not stirred

Get out!

Iz mai private times

i has
a mope

emo cat
wishes u
wud leave

i has a hat

burrito cat

needs moar cheez plzz

Ugh…bachelor pads.
Call me when you
duz lawndry

caffeine crash

i has it

insert cheezburger

doorcat

saw what u did there

party cat

iz partied out

Made in Yew 1999
© Inter IKEA 14
PQM
700 17238
IKEA®
0739

kaat furry doorstop by IKEA

designer sven fuzzybottom

do want

ANGRY KAT

NO LIKES WHEN

YOU MOCKS HIM

faces

or

vase?

conjoined kittehs

hope 2 b separated somday

coffee iz
reddee!!1!

no camras

kthxbai

great night

I'll call you, k?

atlas cat

can always finds u

KITTEH CAN HAS

PERSONAL
SPACE?!

where mah cheezburger?!

grab my paw if you wantz to live

time warp kitteh
is phasing out

I tink we haz a mowse problum…

This won't
end up on the
internet
will it?

oh here's ur problum

dis car is a tabl

after face lift

u do mah nose.

dis doesn't concern u

move along

nite nite bunneh

c u in teh mornin!

DIS NOT RIGHT KIND

BUT I EETED ANYWAY

BUFF Cat

is overcompensating

going
somewheres?

o ur floor
so much awe-
sum!!!1!

litez
poken me
all over

NEED MOAR HOTPOCKETS!

NO.

Solar powered Kitteh

iz rechargin

TEH CRINKLY NOIZE

ITZ FANTASTIC!!1

**new
happy meal
toyz**

**iz been in
there
for dayz**

papr
covers rock

relaxashun
ur doin it rite

MAIM

STUN

smug kitteh

iz pleased wit
own acheevments

ceiling cat iz watching u

CEILING CAT
omnomnishent kitteh who
lives in ur ceiling and observs

ur persunal habitz

i has a flavr

a drinking problum

i has it

narcissistic kitteh

cant get enuf

bidness up front

party in teh back

quiet cat

plots
revenge

vishuns of teh cheezburgers

dancin in mah hed

invisible
upright bass

fly
u foolz!!

I don't know
what hapn 2 ur dog

im on ur table

performin mitosis

refleckshun cat iz spoooky

i haz
a pillo

i haz
a blanket

blastoff

fail

needz 5/16 shoe rench

K let me
reech it

I HATE LOLCAT CAPTION, PLZ STOP

Thx

We would like to thank Ben and Emily Huh and the burger team of Seattle; Kenta and Li-anne of www.otmur.com and their two kids Sammy and Pepper (see illustration) for their fun artwork and cute drawings; Citron & Deutsch, for guidance and patience; Hector Gray of Incrediballistic, for coding the cheezburger factory; MJ, the kissing ninja; Photobucket; WordPress!; Matt, for giving us a chance; Lloyd, for answering our e-mails at 4 A.M.; Barry, for fixing CSS/PHP bugs; Sam + Joseph + Gordon and the rest of the Automattic team; Anil Dash, for his poignant synopsis of what cheezburgers mean to cats; Xeni Jardin and Boing Boing for finding humor in the insane; David McRaney, for thinking hard and writing harder; Scott Beale of Laughing Squid, for always filtering his photos for the best shots; Gordon McNaughton of the original lolcat builder; Barce, the code ninja, Kitty de Medici, queen of captions, Sara Snee and the Flickr Can Has Cheezburger group, and all lolbrarians, for collecting and contributing caps; friends at Catster + Dogster; Chris + Wil at Spunge; Brunetto T-shirts; JS-Kit, the best rating engine; Gmail and 25GB expanded storage; Firefox 2 + Tab Mix Plus, for saving our lives and cluttering our minds; cat lovers around the world; and **IMPACT FONT**. Special thanks to Patrick Mulligan of Gotham for tracking down photo rights and having faith in His Ceilingness (ROR!), Ben Gibson (code name "penben") for covers and layout, and to Kate McKean and Howard Morhaim Literary Agency for understanding the way of the lolz. Finally, we'd like to send a million cheezburgers and thanks to the cats . . . for humoring us.

Kari wishes to thank her mom for her unconditional support, Mr. Fusion for powering her flux capacitor, and Tribble for being tribbly.

Eric sends thanks and love to Mom, Dad, GG, Nana, Moani + Thomas, Martin + Arissa + Kailah, Ian + Brandi, Ashleigh, Carlye, Dezlee, Shannon + Nick + Tania, Thorn + Sasha + Potter, Rick + Daneen + Tam + Pher + Co + Ricky, and 永美子 と 赤ちゃん‼

LOLcat	Thx to
octopus cat is at rest	Cotton by Conrad Baker
OH HAI./ I BUFFED UR FLOOR.	Spencer and Mr. Pouffy by Robin AF Olson (See more at www.coveredincathair.com)
crap	Natalie Fritz
I made you a cookie.../ but I eated it.	Jimmy Leo (www.flickr.com/photos/babykailan)
best sock evar	Kyle by Dayna Abel
RESCUE CAT DO RESCUEZ	Erin Bradley (aka "Miss Information" on Nerve.com)
levitashun./ i has it	Chloe by Marie Sweeten
OH HAI./ I DUN THE SUMZ, WE CAN BUYS NUTHER CHEEZBURGER	Diana Gallagher (www.nottingham-photography.com)
mai preshussss	Janine Roach
SHUN	Matthew Poole
MONORAIL CAT	from teh internets
Monorail cat haz mrgency airbrak	Xena by Barbara Smith
monorail kitteh/ on lift for repares	Amun-Ra by Christina Urban (DivineKittyCat)
IZ MAI OWN HAIRS/ RLY.	anonymous kitteh
EXPLAIN PLZ/ im confusd	Pickle by Steven Pusey
turn the gravity back on, ok hai?	Michael C. Berch
gah!!!/ is full of starz!!!	Kurt Gegenhuber of The Celestial Monochord
thermostat cat/ iz not maed uv monies/ put on a swetter	Lazarus by Ashley Weaver
retrn 2 sendr	Maggie Osterberg (www.flickr.com/photos/mediawench and www.mediawench.com)
Needs halp?/ I canz do fotoshop	Briar-Brae Maugrim of Brenna by Barb Belanger
catmoflage actv8td	Janine Roach
AAAHHHHH See anything??	photo by Giane Portal (www.flickr.com/photos/tofurasfelinas); caption by Leslie Klenke (www.sparethesquid.com)
hey/ i was watching that!	anonymous kitteh
I ARE SERIOUS CAT/ PLZ U STEP INTO MY OFFICE NOW	anonymous kitteh
Naked Guy/ reely freekin me owt	Meemoo by Louise and Ian
aktully Jim what we see here is	Puddi by Audrey
SPY CAM/ installed and functioning	Phoebe Epstein
im in ur hole messin wif ur hed	Julian by Mimi Baker of Dallas, TX
1 2 3 4	Julian by Mimi Baker of Dallas, TX
I C DEAD PEEPS	Lula
OFF TO MOON/ BRB	Giane Portal (www.flickr.com/photos/tofurasfelinas)
emo cat/ sits in corner	Q. McEachern
oh hai been scratchin ur records/ like a dj	Mike and Jenny Lokshin
i hope theyll be gone when i opens mah eyes	The Karaniewsky Family
MYARR!	Pony Lauricella

LOLcat	Thx to
a hedachy/ i has it	Bean and Monkey by Nora Cosgrove-Wagar
banker cat denies ur loan	John Fritz
I beleeves.../ in ceiling cat	Pony Lauricella
I has a punkin flavor	Chino by Kirby and Ashley Schlyer
a best friend... I has it	Raymond Stone
COD/ cat on delivery u pay nao	Bean and Monkey by Nora Cosgrove-Wagar
call for halp i iz stuck for realz this time	Adam Rönnegård ("With cat gone, will there be hope for man?")
invisible guitar solo	Emma by Casey Gardner
I has a job interview	Tjasa&Spela
censor cat/ blocks mature content	Bean and Monkey by Nora Cosgrove-Wagar
nom nom nom	Traci Trapani
litl kiteh has litl noms	Princess Nina Ballerina by Jessie Craig
nom nom nom nom nom	Melanie Northerner
nom de plume	DJ Squeakers by Deb Houghton
cheezburger.../ out dere... sumwheres	Trish Skinner
banana fone/ ringing off teh hook	Chris Pierce
greedy cat wants it all	Indigo by Amber Tull
emo kitteh/ hates pretty things	Cat-a-Clysm by Grant McDonald
evikshun notice SERVED	Charles J. Scheffold
grudge cat iz still ignoring u	James and Jess Boyer
financial advisor cat disapprovs of ur banking methods	Kayla Tackett
HAND ME THE WRENCH!	Natalie Fritz
Come home/ soon plz	Raymond Stone
IN UR QUANTUM BOX.../ ...MAYBE	Kevin Steele; caption by Dan Lurie, geekfriendly.org
gps cat sez u lost.	Kiki by Elizabeth Schoenfeld
for a brief shining moment parrot thought he won	Eisenheim and Miggy
^5	Sam and Max by Karla Anderson
evr hav the feelin/ ur bein watched?	Marzipan by Adam Romig
lazors lockd/ on intrudr	Jeff Bowers
Hello from ebays!/ not wut u xpected?	Rolf Jacobson
couch kitteh/ awaits ur arrival	The Crowe Family and Booger the cat of Dallas, TX
lol/ u peed ur pants	Daniel Lackey and Jill Doornbos
catini shaken not stirred	Frankie by Ashlee Attebery of Arlington, TX
Get out!/ Iz mai private times	Noble by Lili Schmidt
i has a mope	Simba by Judy Parker
emo cat wishes u wud leave.	Hip and the Faber family (Greeting the world from the Netherlands)
i has a hat	Lisa Hill
INVISIBLE LAWNMOWER	Peter Wilson (pwils10@btinternet.com)
invisible superman cape	Ghost by Grace Farstad and Melissa H.

LOLcat	Thx to
invisible violin solo	"Hey Bertha! This is Olga. It pays off being weird. People will accept us for who we are... as soon as we get some masks!"
burrito cat/ needs moar cheez plzz	BarakKhazad
o rly?/ chickn hat agn?	Will Wolff-Myren (www.flickr.com/photos/willwm)
get out/ taking bath	Merry Spratford
Ugh...bachelor pads. Call me when you duz lawndry	Ashley Martineau
caffeine crash/ i has it	Dane Purmalis
tonite/ while u sleep	Camden by Jocelyn Abeldt
kitteh frozen/ must reboot	Indigo by Amber Tull
CAN I PLZ HAS 2 CHEEZBURGERS 3 PUGBURGERS 6 CHIKIN NUGITS NO WAIT MAKE IT 9	Janine Roach
insert cheezburger ------->	Rupert and Ashley Bryan
doorcat/ saw what u did there	Mike, Heather, and Oscar in Covington, GA
party cat/ iz partied out	Cotton by Conrad Baker
hesitant cat/ hesitates	Amy Papa
hai there/ u be my new friend?	Marloes Kleton
kaat furry doorstop by IKEA designer sven fuzzybottom	Dadoopie by Shuhaida and Charles Meekings
cloning ur doin it wrong	Cambria
laser eye surgery ur doin it wrong	Furrari by Kelly George
Facebook/ ur doin it wrong	Jeff Youngstrom (tomecat.com/madtimes)
handpuppet/ ur doin it wrong	Lizz Wilson
k...i redy./ u may add fishes nao	Liz and Todd Burnett with the Weasley Monster
SOME ASSEMBLIES REQUIRED	Agnes
GET OFF LAPTOPZ/ AND FEEDS ME DAMMIT	Bingo by Steve McPherson
do want	Eugene Khudenko
napoleon kitteh/ iz ekspandin teh empyre	Zak by Ann Smedes
ANGRY KAT/ NO LIKES WHEN YOU MOCKS HIM	Miss Priss by David Holmes (thx to Citizens for Animal Protection in Houston, TX)
have you seen.../ my pokemans?	Mary Rose Driskel
faces or vase?	Beth Aslakson (www.bethtoons.com)
chek her out/ she says she's 3 louk moar liek 7 to me!	Courtney Ortiz-Trammell and Oskie, who were introduced to ICHC by Andrew Connolly
do want	Mars, Simo, Lia, and Tony Cooper
conjoined kittehs/ hope 2 b separated somday	Daisy and Jake by Adele Maestranzi
coffee iz reddee!!1!	For Sam Barton, serving our country overseas
no camras kthxbai	Brian & Ashley Martineau
great night/ I'll call you, k?	Victoria Hiley

LOLcat	Thx to
im in ur tube/ blockin ur internets	Martin Cathrae (http://flickr.com/photos/suckamc/)
passwurd plz?/ kthx	Andrew Todd
atlas cat/ can always finds u	Stephane Jeanrenaud
KITTEH CAN HAS/ PERSONAL SPACE?!	Megan Edwards
where mah cheezburger?!	Maren Stewart
grab my paw if you wantz to live	Milli by Laura Poncik
time warp kitteh is phasing out AFK	Idgie by Laura Cox
i tink we haz a mowse problum...	Cambria
This won't end up on the internet will it?	Pony Lauricella
Nosy Neighbor cat/ sees u hidin teh bodies	Grey Bear by Nick and Dara
oh here's ur problum/ dis car is a tabl	Norman by Anne Tudor
after face lift/ u do mah nose.	Nicole Gaddis
dis doesn't concern u/ move along	Kitty Lumpkins by Veronika and Douglas Elsaesser
nite nite bunneh/ c u in teh mornin!	Randy E. Winn (lawyersforwarriors.blogspot.com)
Caturday iz great	Stencer
DIS A JOEK RITE?	Baboo by Amber Edwards
nom nom nom nom	Gracie Grohmann
WAIT I WILL HELPS YOU TYEP! ***	Carmelynn Cole
DIS NOT RIGHT KIND/ BUT I EETED ANYWAY	Jade by Davezilla of Davezilla.com
BUFF Cat/ is overcompensating	Lou Piniella by Andreah Weitz (kickarsedesign@gmail.com)
going somewheres?	Craig Klein
o ur floor so much awe-sum!!1!/ litez poken me all over	Tiger by Lisa Jennings
IM IN UR GARDEN/ SCARIN UR KIDS	Dan Oldre
under ur van/ messin wif ur enjins	Aslaug Svava Jonsdottir and Karl Gunnarsson
im in ur chair watchin ur mooveez	Jonas Voss
im in ur dishwasher/ waitin fer my showr	Jim McClear
i cans lift/ u spot	Molly Kleinman
I regret to inform you that/ ii: p[[[[[[[[[[[[[[[[[[[[[[[[[	Zippy and Noodles by Arron Coates
HALP!!!1!/ Space Invadrz eatin mah bwains %	Fredrik Linge Nygaard
Jus 5 moar minits.../ pleez?	Stimpy by Dan Dalmasso
GIT UR OWN	Gobi by Anne Huys
	Courtney Ortiz-Trammell and Oskie, who were introduced to ICHC by Andrew Connolly
NEED MOAR HOTPOCKETS!	Emma Kowal
NO	Breakfast by Michael and Rhonda Smith
Solar powered Kitteh/ iz rechargin	Mike Blanche
TEH CRINKLY NOIZE/ ITZ FANTASTIC!!1	B.B. by Holly and Andy
nooo, Randy, don't doo it!!!	Fredrik Linge Nygaard
new happy meal toyz/ iz been in there for dayz	Nathan and Mary Rowan

LOLcat	Thx to
papr covers rock	Django and Bailey by Lisa Wohl
polygraph kitteh/ detects deception	Dana Couture, Sue Masel, and Scooter
SIDE EFFECTS INCLUDE:/ MOOD SWINGS LOSS OF APPETITE HAIR LOSS	Jasmine by Rox Church
raised by armadillos	Brett Guillory
NO!1!/ no mor relity tv!1!!	Julie Parker-Garza, Juanita Haggard, and Staci Haggard <3 Teddy!
QWIK!! get mom nao!1!!!/ itz crushin meeee!!1!!	Tiger by Stacy Davidson
relaxashun ur doin it rite	Sable by Eric and Marie Sproul
LAZER SETTINGS:/ KILL STUN MAIM	Robin "Violist" Leung
sleep.../...i needz it	Bart Klein Reesink
smug kitteh/ iz pleased wit own acheevments	Bindi by Katie Graham
ceiling cat iz watching u	From teh internets
Thank u, ceiling cat/ 4 catnip n Caturday	Daniela
Oh, hai ceiling cat./ U scare me.	Gatti by Christina Decurtis
i has a flavr	Mars, Simo, Lia, and Tony Cooper
i darez yu to kross/ no i darez yu to kross	Pony Lauricella
Those who can't do.../ nap.	Bob Cat Bob Bob by Emma-Leigh Johnson
you godda roll wiv it	Raynah Thomas
Iz stuck. Bring hunny.	Women, Fire & Dangerous Things (http://www.flickr.com/photos/wfdt/)
TIS STUF IZ GUDD	Prince by Shawnee Altman
To get prey.../ ...must be liek prey	David and Kathleen Thomas
"toasr is gud nap spot" you sed./ "wut cud go rong?" u sed.	Craig Elliot (www.flickr.com/photos/tjflex/301347804/)
WANT	Jacqueline Collar (chey-sama.deviantart.com)
a drinking problum/ i has it	Mad Max
narcissistic kitteh/ cant get enuf	Angela Buchanan
bidness up front/ party in teh back	Carmelynn Cole
quiet cat/ plots revenge	Candice Frey
so does we has deel?	Candice Frey
may i drive/ use ur blinker!!1!	Porter by Rhonda Hobson
dewey decimal cat is obsolete	Sarah and Robert Ferguson
i gotz to go to teh gim/ meh, tmrw	Loki the Fat (may you live large and prosper)
vishuns of teh cheezburgers/ dancin in mah hed	Ben Gibson
i haz fort/ no tell girlz	Moe by Ryan Keighley
i can has cheezburger to go?	Jackie Fritsche of Eatontown, NJ (www.flickr.com/photos/sis)
maek a note/ u will regret dis atrohcity	Katie Holt
i is ur toy/ try me!	Skye Driggs
invisible upright bass	Daniela
fly u foolz!!	Daniela
getitoff! getitoff!	Daniela
i don't know what hapn 2 ur dog	Cyb3rD0n Architectus

LOLcat	Thx to
ur presentz?/ I ate em	Dylan by Erin Fox and Benjamin Stansfield
invisible kick 2 teh gut	Norman by Holly and Andy
im on ur table/ performin mitosis	Smeagol & Zombie by Holly and Andy
my loogie/ lemme show u it	Bonez by Holly and Andy
refleckshun cat iz spoooky	Ben Gibson
iz 4 u	Mitsu by Lucinda Laveck
halp! it eating meh!!	Benny by Sarah Rogers
LITLE HALP/ kthx!	Thanks to Lifelong Friends in Lago Vista, TX for saving Marlow - Amy Casdorph
HALP/ Mah graviteez iz broked!!1!	Sarah Wilbur
i haz a pillo/ i haz a blanket	Utzu Garcés
blastoff fail	Candice Frey
Grandpa Kitteh/ walk 2 skewl in snow/ uphill bof ways	Gilbert by Jane Tilton
Needz 5/16 shoe-rench/ K let me reech it	Cali and Khmer by Catherine Y. Bae
i HATE LOLCAT CAPTION. PLZ STOP	Rudy by Michele Ferrario (http://www.mferrario.it/latente)